The Easter Bible Storybook

Luke 24:1–16,36; John 20:16; 21:4–7

Jesus died. His body
was put in a cave,
with a stone in front.

Mary and her friends
went to the cave. The
stone had moved!

The cave was empty! Then two angels appeared!

They said, “Jesus is not here. Jesus isn’t dead. He is alive!”

Mary and her
friends were amazed
and very happy.

They ran to tell Jesus' friends the good news: "Jesus is alive!"

Peter and John went to the cave. The cave was empty.

Where was
Jesus? Was he
really alive?

Mary met Jesus
in the garden.
Jesus was alive!

Two friends met
Jesus on the road.
Jesus was alive!

Friends met Jesus
at dinner time.
Jesus was alive!

Peter met Jesus
when he was fishing.
Jesus was alive!

First published 2009, this edition published 2015

ISBN 978 1 78506 187 5

Scripture Union,
207–209 Queensway,
Bletchley, Milton Keynes,
MK2 2EB, England.

Email:
info@scriptureunion.org.uk

Website:
www.scriptureunion.org.uk

British Library Cataloguing-in-Publication Data

A catalogue record of this book is available from the British Library.

Illustration, design and layout: Mark Carpenter Design Consultants

Photography: David Vary

Printed in India by Replika Press Pvt. Ltd.

Scripture Union is an international Christian charity working with churches in more than 130 countries.